Original title:
The Root of All Verse

Copyright © 2025 Creative Arts Management OÜ
All rights reserved.

Author: Samuel Kensington
ISBN HARDBACK: 978-1-80566-622-6
ISBN PAPERBACK: 978-1-80566-907-4

Growing in Silence

In gardens where the whispers play,
The daisies dance, but do they sway?
With roots that giggle underground,
They tell secrets without a sound.

The lettuce laughs when nobody sees,
Telling jokes to the buzzing bees.
While carrots boast about their height,
They pull pranks in the moonlit night.

Layers of Meaning

Like onions wrapped in clever skins,
Each layer hints of silly sins.
The more you peel, the more you find,
A boisterous joy that's quite unkind.

Jokes hidden deep, like roots in soil,
Tend to twist and tangle, coil.
When layered lines come forth to play,
They tickle thoughts in a jovial way.

In the Depths of Emotion

Down in the depths where feelings lie,
A potato dreams of soaring high.
It giggles at the drama near,
While peas roll down in boisterous cheer.

Tomatoes blush with every glance,
Swaying gently, they join the dance.
And when a squash tells a tall tale,
Even the onions laugh and wail.

The Pulse of the Unseen

Beats in the soil that tickle the toes,
Life pulses gently as humor grows.
With roots that jiggle beneath the ground,
They play charades where no one's found.

A rhythm in shadows, a dance so spry,
Where broccoli dreams of a green pie.
In the silence, the fun takes flight,
As plants spin tales under the moonlight.

Echoing in the Silence

In the void where giggles fade,
A whisper danced with shades of jade.
Laughter tickled the quiet air,
As echoes teased without a care.

Mice played tag with shadows bold,
While owls hooted tales of old.
The moon rolled by with a knowing grin,
As silence blushed beneath its spin.

From Ground to Glory

A worm wore glasses, quite the sight,
To read the soil by morning light.
He plotted seeds of dreams untold,
While daisies grinned, both brave and bold.

The potatoes danced in muddy shoes,
With carrots boasting colorful hues.
From earth they sprung, the crops did cheer,
Each root a tale of laughter here.

Charting Unseen Paths

A squirrel sketched maps in nutty ink,
Charting journeys 'round the kitchen sink.
With acorn gems, a treasure hunt,
While sleepy cats just watched and shunt.

Through ceilings, walls, and floors so grand,
He traced a route to neverland.
With giggles echoing down the hall,
Who knew paths could be so small?

Harvest of Heartstrings

Pumpkins chuckled on their vine,
While apples tossed in sweet sunshine.
They played a game of hide and seek,
Each fruit true to their playful streak.

The harvest moon winked with delight,
As corn did dance under the night.
With laughter rippling through the field,
A bounty of joy was surely revealed.

Whittled by the Unsung

The poet scribbles with a grin,
Words tumble out, oh where to begin?
Crafting stanzas from the air,
While squirrels laugh, without a care.

Each line a nugget, shiny, bright,
A verse that tickles, pure delight.
But oh, the puns—too many to count,
In humor's grip, we laugh and flount.

Ascending from the Stillness

From silence springs a raucous tune,
A chorus sung by a sleepy raccoon.
He taps his paws, he struts about,
With flair and zeal, there's never a doubt.

In stillness, words take flight and frolic,
Each chipper phrase, a little symbolic.
With a waltz and jig, they find their place,
As giggles echo, filling the space.

From Darkness to Light

In shadows deep, where rhymes conspire,
A quirky muse ignites the fire.
With silly tricks and goofy rhymes,
She dances forth, transcending times.

The night may hide, yet laughter glows,
As verses bloom like silly shows.
So let's embrace this joyful strife,
And ponder words that dance to life.

The Buried Treasure of Words

In gardens lush, where words reside,
A treasure chest is buried wide.
Inside are giggles, puns galore,
With quirky phrases that we adore.

Digging deep with spoons and shovels,
We uncover wit and silly troubles.
Each line a gem, a playful jest,
In playful prose, we find our quest.

Endings and Beginnings

When one door shuts, it squeaks and moans,
A window opens, full of unknowns.
The classic tale of loss and gain,
Where cows fly high and thoughts fall like rain.

With every end, a start's in sight,
Like socks in a dryer, lost in the night.
Round and round, we twist and twirl,
Who knew life was such a whirl?

Nourishing the Creative Spirit

Feed your mind with snacks galore,
But watch the crumbs tumble on the floor.
A chocolate bar, a piquant thought,
Makes even the dullest ideas sought!

A sprinkle of joy, a dash of glee,
Baking up dreams as sweet as can be.
Stir the pot, don't stir too much,
Or else it could get a little crutch!

Wandering Through the Subtext

Between the lines where whispers hide,
A story lurks, with humor applied.
Like a pickle in a fruit basket's plight,
Oddities dance in the moon's soft light.

Words frolic, wearing silly hats,
Jumping over fences, teasing cats.
Lost in moments we can't quite place,
Reading the humor spread 'cross space.

The Pulse of Inspiration

Inspiration strikes like lightning bolts,
When sitting still, doing absolutely naughts.
Like a chicken crossing just for kicks,
It dances through our minds, pulling tricks.

The spark ignites, ideas take flight,
Like a bird wearing a tux, oh what a sight!
Tickling brains, making them swing,
Crafting laughs from everything!

Depths of Contemplation

In shadows deep, where laughter hides,
A ticklish thought on life's wild rides.
We ponder hard, yet giggles swell,
Who knew that pondering could be so well?

With sticky notes all over the place,
Ideas dance in a silly race.
A thought that spreads, like jam on toast,
Turns serious minds into the toast!

The cat jumps high, the dog barks low,
Each ponderous moment puts on a show.
In every crease of our wrinkled minds,
A chuckle waits that often binds.

So, here we sit with tea and cheer,
Philosophizing through our fear.
Raise a cup, let's make a toast,
To funny thoughts, we love the most!

Intertwined in Emotion

In tangled webs of feeling bright,
We giggle softly through the night.
A tear can roll, a joke can land,
In the circus of life, it's all well-planned.

Chasing crumbs of joy and strife,
Finding humor in daily life.
A glance, a wink, emotions flow,
Laughter's the bridge we often know.

As feelings twist, they tickle the brain,
So don't you frown, embrace the rain.
For every sorrow that's held too tight,
A lighter heart brings pure delight.

With every hug, with every smile,
We wrap our lives in a quirky style.
So dance in feelings, take a chance,
Let laughter lead this wild romance!

Veins of Thought

Thoughts that bounce like rubber balls,
In tangled mazes, laughter calls.
Ideas sprout like weeds in spring,
Oh, let the funny moments cling!

A question asked, a funny face,
We stumble on at a comical pace.
In every ponder, silly and sweet,
A hearty chuckle can't be beat.

Veins of thinking twist and turn,
Making memories that brightly burn.
So let us wander through zany paths,
Where logic laughs, and reason baths.

Hypotheses wrapped in playful jest,
A game of thoughts, we love the best.
So stick your tongue out, what's the fuss?
In the dance of ideas, let's make a fuss!

The Wellspring of Creativity

In the fountain of whimsy where ideas flow,
Creativity's seeds are set in tow.
Splashing colors in a parody dance,
Let's twirl and twirl in this silly trance.

From paint to prose, a comic spree,
Imagination grows like a grand old tree.
Each branch a story, each leaf a joke,
Bursting forth in giggles, what a bloke!

The zany whispers in the mind's tight space,
Do acrobatics, find the face.
Bouncing thoughts like a cheerful ball,
It's art and laughter that enthrall.

So dip your brush, and start to play,
In this well of fun, let worries sway.
With every splash, a smile ignites,
For creativity blooms in funny flights!

Birthed by Shadows

In the dark where giggles play,
Laughter bloomed in shades of gray.
Whispers danced on sneaky feet,
Socks mismatched is quite the treat.

Creativity hides away,
Where shadows laugh and children sway.
It curls like cats on winter nights,
Chasing dreams and playful sights.

A sneaky shadow made a friend,
Wrote poetry that would not end.
With pencils dipped in midnight ink,
The world awoke, or so we think.

From corners crept a silly grin,
As doodles burst and scribbles spin.
In the darkness, no one's lame,
All the shadows share their fame.

Cultivating Dreams in the Dark

In the hallowed halls of snores,
Dreams are planted, never bored.
Monsters wear the silliest hats,
While fairies strut in fuzzy spats.

With sleepy eyes and pillows stacked,
The garden grows though plans are whacked.
Giggling gnomes with watering cans,
Drench desires for second chances.

Awake! The night has dreams to sow,
Dancing on toes, oh what a show!
In these plots where nonsense reigns,
Laughter sprinkles like summer rains.

So cultivate and tend with care,
Each silly thought, a truth to share.
In shadows deep, with hearts so stark,
We find our joy, our dreams embark.

The Well of Creation

A well so deep where giggles flow,
Creativity's hidden show.
With each splash, ideas soar,
Monkeys dance just by the door.

Dive on in, don't hesitate,
Splashing colors, it's first-rate!
Pudding pops and silly pies,
Flavors that will mesmerize.

With every turn, the well spins round,
Unlikely treasures will be found.
A tuba played by sneaky mice,
And jellybeans that roll like dice.

So come equipped with nets and jars,
To catch the dreams that fly like stars.
In a world where laughter's free,
The well of creation calls to thee.

Seeds of Imagination

Planting seeds in minds so bright,
Sprouts of thought take joyful flight.
Dandelions wearing specs,
Grow up tall with funny necks.

They twist and twirl with words in tow,
In gardens where the oddest grow.
Imaginations run amok,
In pots that spark a silly shock.

With watering cans of giggles wide,
We nurture tales that twist and glide.
Oh what sprout's about to bloom?
Giggling unicorns in every room.

So scatter seeds, let laughter roam,
In every heart, we find a home.
From tiny thoughts to grand displays,
In gardens wild, we'll spend our days.

Birthplace of Harmonic Thoughts

In a land where rhymes take flight,
Words dance around, oh what a sight!
Silly squirrels compose their tunes,
While frogs croak under the laughing moons.

Rabbits write while sipping tea,
Chasing shadows, wild and free.
Juggling puns upon their heads,
Making sure that no one treads.

A parrot squawks in perfect verse,
Leaving poets in a curse.
They write and scribble, oh so fast,
Yet their blunders always last.

But here in this whimsical place,
Every giggle finds its space.
Creativity's a merry jest,
Where nonsense reigns, and we're all blessed.

Ties that Bind Creativity

In a world where thoughts unite,
Socks and shoes just can't sit tight.
Colors clash, but who cares, right?
Painted llamas take to flight.

Tangled yarn with tangled minds,
Knitting dreams of all the kinds.
Silly hats that wobble tall,
Make everyone burst out in a brawl.

Creatives gather, plotting schemes,
In bubbles filled with giggly dreams.
They share snacks and silly jokes,
While pondering the dance of folks.

Balloons tied with string so taut,
Floating high, they twist and rot.
Yet laughter echoes in the breeze,
Binding hearts with joyful ease.

Cradle of Verses Untold

In a cradle made of rhyme,
Wiggly worms keep perfect time.
Scribbling lines with wiggly feet,
Their poetic dance is quite a feat.

Each stanza spins like a twirling top,
Silly gnomes that never stop.
They toss confetti, sing out loud,
In their verses, they feel proud.

Frogs tap-dance, they croak the beat,
While bumblebees buzz on their feet.
The trees all sway, they join the fun,
Underneath the bright, warm sun.

With ink-stained paws, they scrawl and play,
In this cradle where words sway.
No story's too silly or grand,
Here, every line takes a stand.

Strings of the Cosmic Lyric

In the cosmos, strings are spun,
Creating melodies, oh what fun!
Planets twirl in a wacky show,
While stars all wink and say hello.

Galaxies jive in silly ways,
Playing hopscotch through the haze.
Each comet trails a quirky rhyme,
Adding joy beyond all time.

Aliens with ukuleles strum,
While singing songs of silly sums.
They gather round the cosmic flame,
And shout their verses, none the same.

In this space of tunes and cheer,
Every giggle rocks the sphere.
For in the stars, this truth holds tight,
Life's a song, pure cosmic delight!

Traces of the Unseen Muse

In the attic, dust bunnies play,
While poems gather, night and day.
A quill wiggles, a paper sighs,
The muse giggles, as laughter flies.

Beneath the bed, rhymes toss and turn,
Dreams of sonnets, a fire to burn.
From shadows they sneak, in a wink and a nod,
Crafting humor, oh, how they prod!

The Beginning of Every Stanza.

Every stanza starts with a fumble,
Words tumble, stumble, and then they mumble.
Puns parade, wearing silly hats,
Adjectives dance with glittery bats.

From laughter thick, to giggles light,
The verbs play tag, a comical sight.
With each new line, they tickle and tease,
A writing party, aiming to please!

Whispers Beneath the Soil

In gardens below, the pun seeds sprout,
Worms cracking jokes, there's no doubt.
Roots twist and shout, 'We're quite profound!'
While bugs chuckle, digging underground.

The daisies giggle, swaying in sync,
While night crawlers scheme, planning to wink.
Beneath the earth, a comic debate,
Creating chuckles while they wait!

Verses in the Underground

In tunnels of rhyme, where echoes glint,
Verses cavort, with a sly hint.
A limerick leaps over muddy pits,
As wordplay juggles, throwing fits.

Line by line, they trip and race,
With giggles sprouting, it's quite the chase.
A cacophony of joy, they all agree,
In this playful realm, a wild spree!

The Landscape of Longing

In the garden of desire, I plant my dreams,
With watering cans filled with silly schemes.
The daisies dance, the sunflowers giggle,
While I chase my thoughts, they wiggle and wiggle.

Beneath a sky of wishes, I fool around,
The butterflies laugh as they flutter around.
Each regret's a quack, just like a duck,
Floating on ponds of wobbly luck.

I paint my hopes with colors so bright,
Yet trips on garden hoses give me a fright.
The moon laughs softly, the stars roll their eyes,
As I tumble and bumble under night skies.

In this whimsical land, I laugh at it all,
My heart climbs high, then takes a small fall.
For in pretty meadows where I stake my claim,
Even longing's a game, and I'm always the same!

Unfolding from the Depths

From the depths of my heart, a joke takes its flight,
A pun that's been brewing, it's almost all right.
I dig with a shovel, uncover a grin,
Like finding a treasure with a smirk on its chin.

With riddles as roots, I bury them deep,
And wake up the squirrels that tumble from sleep.
As they scatter around, I join in their fun,
Chasing my thoughts like a mischievous run.

In a flowerpot, a cactus named Chuck,
Tells tales of adventure, but they're never good luck.
He pokes at the clouds, insisting they rain,
While I stand beside him, soaked, yet remain.

From down in the depths, where the oddities grow,
A party of giggles begins to overflow.
And as shadows unfold, I dance with the sprights,
In the depths of my heart, all the humor ignites!

Timeless Chords of Creation

On a guitar string, I strum a new rhyme,
While the mice in my attic keep perfect time.
Each note is a giggle, a hiccup, a jest,
As I play my tune, come join the fest!

The orchestra of oddballs starts to appear,
A cat on a tuba and a dog with a beer.
The brass section squeaks, the woodwinds go 'meow',
While I scratch my head, and say, "Holy cow!"

With a melody of laughter, the world spins around,
The fun never stops, it knows no ground.
Echoes of joy leap from note to beat,
As I chase after rhythms that tickle my feet.

In the symphony's heart, where chaos takes flight,
All the right notes become hilariously tight.
With timeless chords ringing, I dance here and there,
In creation's own laughter, there's magic to share!

Branches of the Imagination

In a tree of ideas, I swing and I sway,
Pondering nonsense as I giggle all day.
The leaves whisper secrets, the bark tells a tale,
While I climb up each branch without fear of fail.

There's a parrot named Guffaw that squawks out my name,
With feathers of mischief, he's totally lame.
Yet together we conjure the funniest sights,
Turning moments of dullness into pure delights.

Each branch I explore is a leap into fun,
Where worries are jokes that can't weigh a ton.
I swing like a monkey, I hang like a clown,
On branches of dreams in an upside-down town.

In the forest of whim, where laughter abounds,
I find joy in the nonsense that endlessly sounds.
So come climb with me, let's reach for the skies,
In this tree of imagination, we'll break all the ties!

Breathing Life into Thought

In a garden where ideas sprout,
Thoughts wiggle and twist about.
A seed of laughter finds its ground,
And makes the ordinary profound.

The sun shines bright on quirky dreams,
While the moon chuckles with silver beams.
Flowers yawn and stretch their stems,
As words dance and play like gems.

The breeze carries giggles far and wide,
Each turn of phrase, a joyous ride.
Roots tickle the soil, what a sight!
In the funny farm of day and night.

So breathe with whimsy, let thoughts take flight,
In this playful world, everything feels right.
With every chuckle, let your heart bloom,
In the garden where ideas find their room.

Dance of the Roots

In the earth, a party's begun,
Roots are dancing, oh what fun!
They jiggle and wiggle, twist with glee,
Underneath, the roots decree.

They form a conga line so long,
With roots tapping to nature's song.
Worms join in, creating a beat,
While beetles bring their little feat.

Each tap and shuffle shakes the ground,
As whispers of joy swirl all around.
With every downward step they dig,
Creating a rhythm that's oh so big!

And when the rain begins to pour,
The roots kick up and shout for more.
In the dance of life from beneath the sod,
They groan with laughter, any time, any odd.

Inked in the Embrace of Nature

Quills dipped in the laughter of trees,
Nature scribbles words with ease.
Leaves flutter like pages, bright and bold,
Telling stories of tales untold.

The flowers paint verses in vibrant hues,
As bees join in with buzzing cues.
A butterfly flits, creating a rhyme,
In the ink of petals, catching time.

With each stroke, the sky bursts with cheer,
As clouds opt for silly shapes, my dear!
The sun doodles smiles that chase away gloom,
While the breeze whispers secrets from nature's room.

In this masterpiece of laughter and glee,
The canvas of life is wild and free.
So dip your quill in the playful air,
And let nature's humor strip you bare!

The Seedling's Journey

A tiny seed with dreams so grand,
Sets out on a journey, hand in hand.
With a sprinkle of dirt and a kiss of rain,
It giggles as it begins to train.

Through cracks in the sidewalk, oh the thrill!
It stretches and yawns with a wobbly will.
With every push, it giggles in cheer,
Saying, "Look at me, I'm growing here!"

Sunbeams tickle its tiny leaves,
As the winds rustle with whispered reprieves.
The world is vast and funny too,
For what's more silly than a seedling's view?

So up it goes, into the blue,
With aspirations and tales to imbue.
A reminder to all, take a chance,
In life's funny game, let's all dance!

Dreams Taking Flight

I saw a cat in a tiny hat,
Dancing round a bowl of spaghetti.
It claimed to be a famous diplomat,
But I think it just liked being petty.

A dog in shoes chased a rubber duck,
Barking loudly like it was pure gold.
The duck quacked back, oh what a pluck!
Their war of words was quite bold.

A bird on a broom flew past my chair,
Singing tunes just for a laugh.
It sought out a cloud, unaware
That it needed more than a photograph.

Then came a goat with a ukulele,
Strumming awkwardly, looking quite hip.
It sung of cheese, oh so freely,
As I sat and took another sip.

Sonnet in the Soil

In a garden, flowers wear silly hats,
They hold a meeting every afternoon.
The daisies gossip, while old cats sat,
  Bringing echoes of an ancient tune.

The dirt claims to be a scholar wise,
But it really just likes to stick around.
A worm wearing glasses starts to rise,
Saying, "I dig deep, not just on the ground!"

Butterflies fly in a disco dance,
Confetti from petals starts to rain.
They flirt with bees, giving romance a chance,
While ants grumble, complaining about the train.

To laughter they sway, in the soil's embrace,
Where each root has secrets, or so they proclaim.
A comedy show in this earthy place,
Turning plants into the life of the game.

Taps from the Underground

In the underworld, where the gophers play,
They host a talent show with much delight.
A mole recites poems in a wise way,
While worms perform magic, a sight quite bright.

Rats wear bow ties and drink from a cup,
Sipping tea, feeling rather refined.
But their table manners could use a clean-up,
Their crumbs fly around, oh so unconfined!

A hedgehog comes out with a saxophone,
Playing jazz that could wake the dead.
Tunnels echoing beats, a wild tone,
As creatures groove, nodding their head.

In this burrowed cabaret of cheer,
They laugh at the surface, unaware of the sun.
It's clear that underground is where joy is near,
Their antics remind us that life is fun.

The Poetry of Existence

Oh, the fridge, a poet of snacks and creams,
Whispers odes to leftovers on the shelf.
The light flickers while it softly dreams,
Of a world where ketchup can be itself.

In the hallway, shadows strike a pose,
Competing for the title of best disguise.
They giggle and stretch, but nobody knows,
That two dust bunnies hide with winning lies.

A toaster pops up, proud of its toast,
Shouting glory, like a champ in a race.
The jam tries to spread, feeling like a boast,
While the butter just melts, like a silly face.

Life's absurd, in this kitchen delight,
Where all seem to play, with humor to boast.
In the daytime, or through the night,
Existence is poetry; let's raise a toast!

Roots in Rhythm

In the garden of words, they dance along,
With giggles and wiggles, they feel so strong.
Beneath the loud laughter, beneath the bright sun,
They twist and they turn, oh, how they have fun!

From puns like a vine that climbs up a tree,
To rhymes that will tickle like a soft bumblebee.
With each little quirk, they bounce and they play,
In the soil of our thoughts, they brighten the day.

Oh, the roots intertwined, beneath giggles they grow,
In a world full of jokes, they put on a show.
They tease and they tumble, with jesters' delight,
In the heart of this garden, all laughter feels right.

With wiggles and jumbles, they find a way through,
In the melody of nonsense, there's always a clue.
So let's dance with the words, let our spirits take flight,
For in the roots of our humor, it's always all right.

Petals of Metaphor's Garden

Petals are prancing, a colorful sight,
In a garden where metaphors take flight.
A daisy of dialogue, a lily of laughs,
Each flower a story, with quirky paths.

Sunflowers salute with a wink and a nod,
While tulips speak softly, but aren't at all odd.
In the bloom of confusion, bright colors abound,
With jokes growing wild in the soft, fluffy ground.

The thorns tell a tale, but oh, not too clear,
They poke and they prod, but we hold them dear.
In the whirl of giggles, this garden's a feast,
Where petals of puns could make even cows ceased.

With each silly bloom, we sip on some tea,
Reflections of laughter, oh how can it be?
For in this sweet garden, our imaginations play,
Amongst petals and verses that brighten the day.

Timeless Echoes of Expression

Echoes of laughter bounce in the hall,
With whispers and chuckles, they stumble and sprawl.
In the chamber of words, like monkeys they swing,
Each jest a reminder of what joy can bring.

The clock ticks a rhythm, which we dance and hum,
Taking leaps with our verses, we welcome the fun.
Should we trip on a pun, oh, what a delight,
In the echoes of laughter, we soar to new height.

With whispers of joy, the feedback is bright,
Playing tag with the phrases, left and right.
In the dance of expressions, we find our own place,
With each laugh a ripple, it's joy we embrace.

So let's play these echoes through time and through space,
In the symphony of humor, we all find our grace.
A chorus of giggles, where all hearts align,
In the timeless arena, our spirits will shine.

Layers of Language Unfolded

With layers of chaos, our words intertwine,
In a tapestry silly, where jokes brightly shine.
First layer is laughter, then comes the surprise,
Like onions of humor, they bring tears to our eyes.

The second layer wobbles, oh look at it sway,
With rhythms of nonsense that dance and play.
In this fold of confusion, we find what is true,
Like waffles and syrup, mixed up just for you.

Peeling back the layers reveals little gems,
With each quirky twist, we delight in the hems.
The threads of our tales wrap around our feet,
In a whirl of giggles, our lives become sweet.

So let the layers unfold, let's not rush the show,
For in every silly twist, there's always a glow.
In the fabric of language, let laughter be bold,
In layers of joy, let each story be told.

Germination of the Heart

In a garden where dreams collide,
Seeds of laughter love to hide,
Watered by jokes, they start to sprout,
Tickling roots, they twist about.

With every chuckle, petals bloom,
A bouquet of giggles fills the room,
Bumbling bees join in the dance,
Fumbling steps lead to romance.

Worms wear hats and join the fun,
Making rounds under the sun,
Caterpillars laugh in delight,
While butterflies prepare for flight.

So plant a smile, let laughter grow,
In this garden, feelings flow,
From tiny seeds to giant trees,
Life's a jest with every breeze.

Through the Layers of Language

Words stack up like pancakes high,
Flipping meanings in the sky,
Syrup's tricky, sometimes it drips,
While we giggle through our slips.

Each letter's wearing a silly grin,
Dancing around with a cheeky spin,
Vowels fight with consonants bright,
In a wordy brawl of pure delight.

Puns are sprinkles on this cake,
A dessert made for laughter's sake,
With every twist, a joke unfolds,
Langues jostle, bold yet cold.

So dive deep into this treat,
Where chatter and laughter greet,
Climbing layers, we find our way,
In playful speech, we laugh and play.

Shadows of the Past

Ghosts of laughter haunt the night,
With silly tales that feel so right,
Every story's wrapped in jest,
Past and present, comedy's quest.

Old socks wander, lost and found,
Searching for laughs under the ground,
A distant echo, fade and flare,
Whispers of giggles linger in the air.

Jokes that traveled through time and space,
Find new laughs in an old place,
Silly hats and puns reappear,
As history dances with a cheer!

So let the chuckles echo wide,
As shadows play with hearts inside,
In every story, there's a spark,
Where comedy glows bright in the dark.

Resonating with the Earth

The ground hums with a sly delight,
As laughter springs forth, taking flight,
Roots reach deep for a senseless rhyme,
Tickling earthworms, all in good time.

Mountains chuckle, rivers run fast,
Nature's punchlines forever last,
A breeze whispers secrets, oh so sweet,
While trees tap dance with leafy feet.

Clouds unroll in a playful jest,
Throwing shade as they drift west,
Rain drops giggle in puddles below,
The earth's comedy puts on a show.

So join the symphony of glee,
Feel the joy, wild and free,
In the nature of laughter, we find our worth,
Resonating joyfully with the Earth.

The Well from Which Words Spring

In the deep of night, words get a drink,
They wiggle and giggle, far too fast to think.
A squirrel wears a hat, dancing on a log,
While the moon plays chess with a witty frog.

Each line is a noodle, slippery and long,
Twirling with laughter, like a playful song.
The ink spills secrets, oh what a mess!
As the pen tries to juggle, in a fancy dress.

From shadows they tumble, into the light,
Chasing the giggles, oh what a sight!
A circus of verses, waiting to cheer,
Each rhyme that dances, spreading good cheer.

So dip down your bucket, take a wild sip,
From this wondrous well, let your stories flip.
A fountain of fun, where nonsense does spring,
In the splash of the words, let your laughter ring.

Shadows and Light of Storytelling

With shadows that wiggle, stories come alive,
A cat wearing glasses, thinking, "How do I thrive?"
The light flickers softly, like a hint at a joke,
While a fish on a skateboard begins to provoke.

A whale hums a tune, under the surface so deep,
While the sun's golden giggles tickle the sheep.
Characters dance wildly, in a playful parade,
As the storyteller juggles, with joy unafraid.

Oh, the tales we can spin, like candy on a thread,
Where a pickle and donut hold court in your head.
Each shadow a canvas, each light a bright spark,
Join in the rhythm, let's park in the lark!

From the giggles of words, a vast world takes flight,
Where quirks mix with silence, and laughter ignites.
So gather your thoughts, let the stories unfold,
In this laugh-filled realm, where imagination is bold.

Threads of Midnight Musings

In twilight's embrace, thoughts start to stroll,
A rabbit in pajamas, tipsy but whole.
With threads of silver, they weave through the night,
Knitting up dreams with laughter so bright.

A squirrel in ballet shoes, spins with delight,
While the stars twinkle back, all dressed in white.
Each thought is a noodle, looped in a dance,
As the moon whispers secrets, giving dreams a chance.

Oh, midnight, you rascal, where nonsense takes flight,
With penguins on bicycles circling the light.
Each thread tells a story, so wild and so free,
Where the silly and witty dance gaily with glee.

So come join the musings, let your mind play a tune,
With shadows of whimsy, and laughter's sweet boon.
In the depth of the night, let your thoughts intertwine,
For in threads of the silly, all stories will shine.

The Soul's Silent Palette

In colors of chuckles, the palette does glow,
A paintbrush of giggles, to give it a go.
With splashy creations, absurdity flows,
As the canvas grins wide, with whimsically prose.

A purple koala in slippers so bright,
Is crafting a rainbow, with sheer delight.
While the trees laugh and wiggle, in breezes that tease,
A penguin in sunglasses, enjoying the tease.

The palette's a garden, where silliness grows,
Each stroke a delight, where the laughter just flows.
Mixing the colors, shades beyond measure,
In this crazy world, find your heart's hidden treasure.

So dip in the humor, let joy be your guide,
In the palette of life, you'll find giggles abide.
With each brush of laughter, let your spirit prevail,
In the soul's vibrant canvas, let the joy set sail!

Veins of the Written Word

Words flow like wine, oh what a treat,
Ink spills like juice, can't find my seat.
Scribbles and giggles, napkins in hand,
Poetic disasters, completely unplanned.

A rhyming disaster, a metrical mess,
Lines that don't fit in, causing distress.
My pen takes a trip to a whimsical land,
Where the grammar is shaky, but oh so grand.

Stanzas are towering, like spaghetti spills,
A sonnet's a nightmare, hey, let's get thrills!
Joking with verses, absurdity reigns,
Laughing at language, it eases the pains.

Each verse is a chuckle, a dance on the page,
The quirks of my writing have gone to a rage.
So join in my laughter, it's all in good fun,
These veins of the written, oh boy, they've just begun.

Pathways to Poet's Heart

Hop, skip, and jump down the dotted line,
Poets with quirks often sip on the wine.
They scribble their troubles on napkins for fun,
While searching for rhythms that never get done.

Wandering pathways, oh what a sight,
Finding lost verses in the dead of night.
A rhyme scheme is tripping, just like my toes,
As I trip over syllables, nobody knows.

With each silly stanza, I'm losing my place,
Spinning around in this poetic race.
The heart of a poet is messy, it's true,
Filled with strange metaphors, and maybe some stew.

We chase after laughter, we follow the beat,
Creating odd patterns that can't be discreet.
Pathways that giggle, through valleys and parts,
Lead us – unsteady – to the poet's heart.

Journeys of Ink and Thought

Ink flows like water, but messier still,
Thoughts chase like rabbits, can't catch them at will.
Pages are dancing, they're sliding away,
While I shout at my pen, 'Hey, come back, stay!'

A journey of nonsense, from me to the page,
Words playing hide-and-seek, oh what a stage!
I scribble my dreams, and they laugh in my face,
Oh, what a circus in this poetic space.

The ink spills like secrets, oh what a sight,
My thoughts are like fireworks, they take off at night.
Chasing down laughter in this whimsical race,
Each twist in my journey brings joy to my face.

With every misstep and twist in the plot,
I'll dance with the ink and see what I've got.
Journeys of giggles, and thoughts that are wild,
In the land of the wordplay, I'm the eternal child.

The Fabric of Emotional Verse

Knots in the fabric, a tangle in rhyme,
Emotions run wild, like they're out of time.
I stitch together laughter and sighs that I find,
In this wacky quilt of the poetic mind.

With threads of absurdity weaving a tale,
I pull at the seams, will this ever entail?
Each line is a pattern, so quirky and bright,
The fabric of feelings, a comical sight.

Stitched up with humor, I'll wear it with pride,
These emotions of writing can't stay inside.
So gather around, in this stitch-and-glue show,
The fabric we create, with a laugh and a glow.

In verses of nonsense, the heart starts to stir,
I'll dance 'round the room, in this wacky couture.
Each patch tells a story, a chuckle, a verse,
In this quirky creation, we're all well rehearsed.

In the Cradle of Expression

In a land where giggles grow,
Poets laugh, and rhymes do flow.
With every twist, a pun takes flight,
Witty words dance in the night.

Chasing ideas like a game,
Each line winks, none are the same.
Metaphors in silly hats,
Jokes about the silliest cats.

Verses swirl like cotton candy,
Frolicking thoughts, oh so dandy!
Imagery runs wild, quite gleeful,
Where nonsense takes the role of equal.

So come and play where the jokes do sing,
Life's a circus, let the laughter cling.
In this cradle of fun we find,
The joy of verse, a playful mind.

Subterranean Voices

Down below where roots all meet,
Worms recite in wiggly beat.
Riddles whispered in the soil,
They giggle as they tend to toil.

"Why did the tomato turn red?"
As one would joke in the dirt bed.
The radishes snicker, the carrots chime,
In this underworld, humor's prime.

When daisies bloom, they shrug and sway,
"Roots are funny in their own way!"
Earthworms tease with puns so sly,
While mushrooms chuckle as they try.

Subterranean laughter, oh so sweet,
Making the underground feel complete.
In the depths of the earth, they have their fun,
A funny place where all's well done.

Weaving Through the Roots

Threads of laughter sewn with care,
In the tapestry of air.
Each strand a quip, each loop a jest,
We weave our words and do our best.

Tangled tales and puns galore,
Stories knock on every door.
With needles of humor, we stitch the night,
Creating smiles with pure delight.

The fabric of rhyme stretches so wide,
Bringing giggles that can't be denied.
Knots of irony, bows of fun,
In this craft, all can be spun.

So grab a thread, join the dance,
Let's twirl through stanzas, take a chance.
In the garden where humor grows,
Weaving laughter 'til the sunlight glows.

The Soil of Sentiments

In a patch where feelings sprout,
Funny quirks we laugh about.
Sentiments bloom like daisies bright,
In this patch, it feels just right.

From laughter seeds, we plant each day,
Watering jokes in a silly way.
A compost of puns, rich and deep,
In this soil, we sow and reap.

Witty roots twist in delight,
Tickling tales both day and night.
Personal charm in every sprig,
A joy-filled life, let's dig, dig, dig!

So let's grow with laughter's might,
In the soil of whimsy, everything's bright.
With emotions as flowers, we sing our tune,
In a garden of giggles, 'neath a joking moon.

Ties that Bind the Muse

A pen and paper dance with glee,
Scribbles that giggle, wild and free.
Each word a wiggle, a silly twist,
Who knew that rhymes could be a tryst?

In cups of coffee, ideas brew,
Like frothy bubbles, they pop anew.
With laughter ringing in the air,
Every phrase, a jester's flair.

Jokes that tumble, rhymes in a whirl,
Puns that leap, give scribes a twirl.
As I capture thoughts in quirky ink,
My giggling muse is on the brink.

So chase the scribbles, catch the quips,
Let every line be laughter's trips.
In this wild verse, we all align,
The muse is laughing, all is fine.

The Heart of Language

Words are hungry, munching sounds,
In every corner, laughter bounds.
When syllables trip, they take a leap,
Into the rhythm, no time for sleep.

A funny frog hops in my brain,
Croaking sonnets, it's insane!
With each refrain, the room erupts,
Language tickles and laughs corrupt.

Commas giggle, periods sigh,
Exclamation marks say, "Oh my!"
With every phrase, a chuckle grows,
In the heart of talk, mischief flows.

Just let the words take silly rides,
On this topic, the humor hides.
Language dances, and all is bright,
In the world of verse, we find delight.

Echoes from the Earth

The soil whispers secrets low,
While crickets chirp a tune in tow.
Every seed a story spins,
In earthy laughter, the fun begins.

Roots are tangled, twisting wide,
Like socks lost on the laundry ride.
The ground giggles, with quirks to share,
As dandelions tease the summer air.

A tree trunk jokes with squirrels near,
Chasing shadows, they disappear.
In every breeze, there's a friendly jest,
Nature's comedy is the very best.

So listen closely, hear the cheer,
From all around, the laughs appear.
Echoes bounce from branch to stone,
In this great world, we're never alone.

Threads of Inspiration

In the loom of thought, ideas weave,
Colorful threads that never leave.
With laughter spun through every line,
We create a fabric, oh so fine!

Tangled yarns and silly strings,
The muse prances, and joy it brings.
As stitches yank, a quilt unfurls,
In quirky patterns, laughter swirls.

Each thread a whim, a tale to tell,
In a tapestry of giggles, we dwell.
With needles poking through the fluff,
Creating giggles is never tough.

So take your tools, let's all create,
A woven world where fun is fate.
Inspiration flows, like a merry stream,
Together we'll stitch a happy dream.

Flourish of the Fabled

In a garden of dreams, a gnome takes a nap,
With a hat full of jokes and a comically big map.
He plants seeds of laughter in the soil of delight,
Hoping that whimsies will take joyful flight.

The daisies are giggling, tulips share a grin,
While carrots in shame try to hide their green skin.
The roses, so sassy, throw shade at the breeze,
While the mushrooms are gossiping, down on their knees.

Oh, the soil is rich with tales ever grand,
As veggies converse in their quirky band.
Each sprout and each bloom has a story to tell,
In this fabled garden where laughter does dwell.

Echoed Roots of Melody

Beneath the old oak, the critters convene,
With a banjo, a flute, and a dance routine.
The squirrels go wild, while the raccoons clap,
A symphony brewing, no time for a nap.

The worms start to wiggle, with beats in their souls,
While the birds sing along in high-pitched strolls.
A frog hits the drums—rib-bat, rib-bat,
Creating a ruckus, imagine that!

The roots start to jiggle, the earth sings in tune,
As flowers tango under the light of the moon.
In this concert of nonsense, joy takes its flight,
With melodies ringing till the morning light.

The Undercurrent of Inspiration

In a pond of ideas, the frogs leap with glee,
Skipping stones of thought, oh so carefree.
With splashes of whimsy, they conjure a theme,
As lily pads float on the surface of dreams.

The fish take a dive, they're artists at play,
Creating bright swirls in a splashy display.
While dragonflies giggle, with their wings all a-whirl,
They weave tales of laughter with every twirl.

A turtle in glasses reads poetry wide,
While the minnows swim round, trying to hide.
Inspiration runs deep, from the banks to the stars,
In this whimsical realm, we're all quirky czars.

Bitter Sweet Growth

A cabbage once dreamt to be sweet as a pie,
But grew up with bitterness, oh me, oh my!
The beans told her stories of sugar and spice,
While she frowned and replied, "I'm not that nice!"

The tomatoes once hoped they'd shine like the sun,
But their faces turned red from a joke that was fun.
Each sprout held a grudge, each root had a tale,
Of bitter old rivalries that made them all pale.

Yet through all the squabbles and snarky comebacks,
A salad was born with hilarious cracks.
In dressing of laughter, their flavors unite,
Bitter meets sweet, what a comical sight!

Whispered Inspirations in Bloom

In a garden where giggles grow,
Ideas dance like worms in a row.
Puns sprout up with such delight,
Colors clash in joyful sight.

The daisies gossip, the roses grin,
As rhymes twist and twirl like a spin.
A bumblebee hums a silly tune,
While the sun wears a hat like a cartoon.

Frogs play chess with a wink and a croak,
And daisies chuckle at every joke.
With each petal drop, a giggle bursts,
As laughter blooms and never thirsts.

So come, oh friend, join the jolly jest,
In this garden, we'll never rest.
We'll write our verses, both mad and bright,
Under the moon's unending light.

The Canvas of Expression

A splash of paint, a brush's sway,
Blue cows dance, but only in May.
The sun wears shades; such a sight,
Clouds drift by, but they're all polite.

Canvas stretched under giggly skies,
Where kittens exchange the best of lies.
Colors fight in a vibrant brawl,
But all in fun, we welcome them all.

Brush strokes giggle, as they sneak peek,
In a world where the daffodils speak.
Silly shapes of fish in a hat,
Join the swirl of all things flat.

Let's paint a world devoid of gloom,
Where laughter shines and colors zoom.
Every creation, a chuckle in sight,
On this canvas, our spirits take flight.

Melodies Beneath the Surface

In a pond where the frogs serenade,
Beats drop like a fish masquerade.
With a splash of laughter, tunes abound,
Every melody shakes the ground.

Silly crickets hold concerts at night,
Singing duets that feel just right.
The turtles join with a clumsy sway,
While bubbles burst in a jazzy play.

Underwater echoes of giggles swirl,
As the goldfish show off their twirl.
A symphony of winks and cheer,
Every note tickles the ear.

So dive right in, embrace the beat,
Dance like nobody's on their feet.
In this pond, the music flows,
As laughter bubbles and joy just grows.

The Nexus of Narrative Flow

In a world where stories bounce and play,
Characters prance in a merry way.
Plot twists jive, they spin around,
In comical tales once lost, now found.

A hero trips over their own cape,
While villains grin, plotting their escape.
Dialogue sparkles like soda pop,
With every word, the laughter won't stop.

Every chapter a leap into fun,
With quirks and quips, they run and run.
So grab your quill, let's write a tale,
Where silly antics will never fail.

Join this romp through a whimsical land,
With every turn, a slapstick band.
In the hub of humor, we create and flow,
In tales of laughter, watch our spirits grow.

Where Poetry Takes Root

In gardens where the rhymes do sprout,
Words wiggle like a worm, there's no doubt.
They twist, they turn, all around they twine,
A dance of laughter, a draught so fine.

With every seed of thought we share,
A giggle grows, it fills the air.
The puns, like flowers, bloom and tease,
In this rhyming patch, we do as we please.

We water jokes with wit and cheer,
And watch them blossom year by year.
The silly sprouts in every line,
Unroot all frowns, let joy entwine.

So grab your spade, it's time to dig,
Let's plant some puns, let's dance a jig!
In this poetic plot so bright,
Where laughter grows, it feels so right!

Beneath the Surface of Thought

In caverns deep where ideas hide,
A troll of humor tries to abide.
He juggles thoughts, a jester bold,
With punchlines wrapped in tales untold.

Beneath the thoughts, a tickle stirs,
Nonsense dances like happy furs.
We dig for gold, but find a joke,
That makes us laugh until we choke.

What lurks below, we cannot know,
Maybe a pun or a witty show.
So let's dive deep, past gloom and dread,
And surface with a chuckle instead!

The depths of wit, a treasure trove,
In silly caves, the spirits rove.
So join the quest, let's twist and play,
Beneath the thought, we've found our way!

Harvesting Words from the Abyss

In fields so dark where whispers creep,
We gather words while others sleep.
With baskets full of puns and glee,
Harvesting laughs, just you and me.

We plow through soil of silly rhymes,
Unearthing giggles, olden times.
The roots run deep, but what a yield,
Each chuckle's worth, our hearts are healed.

The abyss below, it sings a tune,
Of jesters dancing 'neath the moon.
With every scrape of shovels bright,
We plant our jokes and share the light.

So come and join this merry spree,
Unleash your laughs, be wild and free.
In fields where humor's never missed,
Let's bake our fun in friendship's crust!

The Essence of Expression

With every word, we craft a laugh,
Like sculptors shaping jokes with craft.
The essence flows from heart to pen,
A giggle squeezed from deep within.

Expressions bloom, a garden rare,
With every pun, we thread a care.
Laughter bursts like colors bright,
Painting joys on canvas white.

Each line a sip of fizzy fun,
A hearty chuckle, oh what a run!
So raise your glass of rhymes and cheer,
To joy expressed, through verse we steer.

In every stanza, love's embraced,
With humor's touch, our hearts we placed.
So pen your thoughts, let laughter flow,
In essence, joy will always grow!

The Pulse of Poetic Souls

In a world of rhymes and fluffs,
Words tickle like the silliest cuffs.
Jumping jacks of jumbled thoughts,
Playful whispers that time forgot.

Giggles dance on paper sheets,
Silly verses with wobbly beats.
They trip and fall, oh what a sight!
Making lovers of laughter unite.

Crafting humor from the mundane,
With each line, wit runs like rain.
A chuckle here, a grin over there,
Lyrical antics fill the air.

So let's embrace this playful art,
As words bounce and joy departs.
With every giggle, a story flows,
In this funhouse where poetry grows.

Origins of Written Dreams

In scribbles found on old book spines,
Lies the birth of silly signs.
Once serious thoughts now twirl about,
Like knotted socks in a playful route.

Harking back to paper trails,
Where dreams took flight with chicken tails.
A feathery pen and ink so bright,
Wrote tales of socks lost in the night.

In every line, a jest unfolds,
Of mismatched shoes and stories told.
From moody scribbles to laughter's feast,
We prank the tomes; words never ceased.

So gather round, let humor reign,
In every quirk, there's bliss to gain.
With pen in hand, unleash your schemes,
In this wild world of written dreams.

Heartstrings of Creative Spirit

Strings of laughter pull and twist,
My heartbeats dance as words insist.
They sashay through the silliest arts,
Tickling funny bones and hearts.

With every strum of cheeky lines,
Joyful echoes of ancient pines.
A tale of socks and jumbled shoes,
All woven into poetic cues.

When words collide, the magic sparks,
In friendly brawls of made-up larks.
One's a cat, the other a mouse,
Living tales inside a fun house.

Embrace the jests, let laughter ring,
Creative spirits take to wing.
In each odd verse, a treasure lies,
To tickle souls and light the skies.

Chronicles in Every Line

Chasing tales like puppies do,
In every corner, giggles brew.
Chronicles woven with mismatched threads,
Of dancing dreams and silly spreads.

Each line a quirk, a slip, a slide,
Adventures riding a comical tide.
A watermelon in a tuxedo waits,
To entertain and open gates.

The fun of words is hard to curb,
When laughter rolls and minds disturb.
With every punchline, a twist anew,
In the grand saga of the goofy crew.

So gather your scribbles, don't be shy,
Let's laugh until we almost cry.
In every tale, a spark divine,
Lies a world of wonder in every line.

Echoes of Untold Stories

In a corner of the world so small,
Lies a gnome with a love for a ping-pong ball.
He spins tales of grandeur, a knight with a flair,
But really, he's just lost his golden spare.

The trees around chuckle, they sway in delight,
As he challenges shadows to dance in the night.
A frog joins the chorus, singing out loud,
While squirrels take bets, cheering for his crowd.

His stories grow wild, like weeds in the sun,
Mixing up legends, oh what twisted fun!
The punchline arrives with a flick of his hat,
And all of his secrets? They fit in a spat!

Laughter escapes his tiny gnome mouth,
As he reminisces of journeys down south.
But the ball rolls away, oh what a disgrace,
He'll just spin it back with a grin on his face.

The Hidden Source of Rhythm

In the heart of the kitchen, a spatula sings,
To the rhythm of pancakes and other such flings.
The blender joins in, with a whirr and a hum,
While the fridge holds its breath, feeling quite glum.

An old teapot joins, bubbling with glee,
Dancing on counters, oh what a spree!
But a rogue spoon rebels, starts to take flight,
Clashing with forks in a bumpy delight!

They jive and they wiggle, a merry old crew,
Mixing up beats in a breakfast brew.
Yet amidst all the chaos, a whisk tumbles down,
And giggles erupt in the apron's crown.

With flour on noses, they cheer and collide,
This kitchen's a party, no need to hide!
In this joyful mess, the rhythm remains,
A symphony of laughter and pancake refrains.

A Tangle of Feelings

There once was a sock who felt quite alone,
Searching for mates in a land of unknown.
With a tear in his seam and a hole in his toe,
He set off for friendship, with nowhere to go.

He tripped over yarn, tangled in threads,
Fell into a basket of sleepy old beds.
There he found slippers, both fuzzy and warm,
Together they plotted on how to transform.

They staged a revolt, the lonely sock crew,
They crafted a plan, oh what a breakthrough!
With mismatched shoes on, they danced through the night,

Their laughter ignited the room with pure light.

Once lonely and lost, now a party in style,
The sock and his friends went the extra mile.
Feeling a tangle is often quite grand,
When you find joy together, hand in hand!

Beneath the Canopy of Thought

Beneath a tall tree with thoughts flying high,
Sat a bird wearing glasses, oh my, oh my!
He pondered the secrets of worms in the ground,
While squirrels discussed the best acorn they found.

The leaves whispered truths, but they twisted and turned,
And the more that they spoke, the more he discerned.
With each passing cloud, he furrowed his brows,
As the world spun around like an old, silly clown.

He pondered why crickets sang their night song,
And what in the world could possibly be wrong.
With a quill and a notepad, he scribbled away,
Crafting nonsense that brightened his day.

In a world full of questions, he strove to explore,
Laughter and joy were what he adored.
Beneath the vast canopy, through giggles and sighs,
He discovered that seeking was the greatest prize.

The Grounded Spirit of Art

In the soil where ideas sprout,
Laughter bubbles, no doubt!
Colors dance in a wild spree,
Paintings giggle, can't you see?

Crayons fight in a box so bright,
Each one claiming, 'I'll be the light!'
Yet in chaos, a masterpiece forms,
As we embrace creative norms.

Brushes tickle the canvas fair,
Every stroke, a playful dare!
Artistry sings in whimsical tones,
As laughter echoes through the stones.

So let's splash whimsies everywhere!
Watch the world brighten with flair!
For in this merry, colorful dance,
Lies the heart of our wild romance.

Nourishment for the Soul

In the garden of giggles, we grow,
Feasting on joy, don't you know?
Laughter seasoned with a pinch of spice,
A buffet where silliness is nice.

Here's a plate of puns, hot and fresh,
Each one serving up a fun mesh.
Sprinkled with kindness, a dash of cheer,
Satisfaction enough to persevere.

Fruit of dreams, ripe and bright,
Biting into hope feels just right!
Delicious banter, served with a smile,
Come join the feast, oh, stay for a while!

So nourish your spirit, take a bite,
In this quirky garden, all feels right.
For life's a spread, both weird and sweet,
With laughter as the soul's true treat.

Traces of Ancient Voices

Whispers echo from paths of yore,
Tickling the ears, oh, what a roar!
Ancient jesters, in shadows, blend,
Leaving footprints where giggles ascend.

Stories tumble through the playful air,
Noses twitching like rabbits in their lair.
Echoes of laughter from times long gone,
As the past dances into the dawn.

Marble statues cracking a grin,
Mirth and mischief are never thin.
With each chuckle from history's page,
The ages collide in a joyful stage.

In this curious game of rhyme and jest,
The old spirits sing, never at rest.
So raise a glass to the wittiest trace,
And join in the chaos, a merry embrace!

The Fountain of Whispers

Beneath the trees, a fountain springs,
Gathering secrets, laughter it brings.
Each droplet dances, a story it shares,
Tickling thoughts lost in our cares.

Rippling giggles, the water flows,
Whispers of fun where mischief grows.
Splashing wit like a joyous crowd,
Here imagination is unbowed.

Tales spun from the fountain's grace,
Painting smiles on every face.
So come, take a drink from this stream,
And revive the wonders of each dream.

For in this fountain, all are free,
To laugh and dance, just you and me.
Let's fill our hearts with joyful cheer,
For the whispers unite us, far and near.

Dense Canopies of Thought

In a forest of ideas, I lost my way,
Chasing squirrels of wisdom, come out to play.
Branches confuse me, I trip on a vine,
Even the mushrooms are starting to whine.

A tree said to me, 'You're thinking too hard,'
As I pondered its bark, feeling rather charred.
Critters laughed loudly, they danced on my head,
Claiming I'm lost, should have stayed home in bed.

Rain fell like thoughts, each drop in a whirl,
Mixed up my musings, then gave me a twirl.
I gathered my wits, all soggy and wet,
Switched to a puddle, no need for regret.

With roots of absurdity, I found my way back,
Worms on a mission, they paved the way, slack.
Underneath all that green, a laugh starts to grow,
In this dense canopy, thoughts overflow.

Resilience of Imagination

A cat in a hat read a book on a bough,
With pages so silly, I wondered just how.
Wizards and fairies, they danced in a line,
All while the dog tried to sip on some wine.

Imaginations bounce like a trampoline,
Rabbits jump high, look at them careen.
Ideas are robust, they don't mind the fall,
Like jellybeans bouncing, they giggle and sprawl.

An octopus offered me pearls made of cheese,
Said, "Taste these delights, you'll be sure to please."
I laughed till I cried, oh what a wild treat,
In this whimsical world, my heart felt the beat.

With minds like balloons, we float and we drift,
Surreal and resourceful, miracles shift.
For laughter's the key, it's our clever disguise,
Resilience in fun plays, oh what a surprise!

Silent Murmurs of the Mind

In corners of quiet, where thoughts like to hide,
A voice whisper giggles, 'Come take me for a ride!'
Socks with no partners dance under the bed,
While dreams dressed as clowns trampoline on my head.

I heard a balloon talking to a tin can,
Sharing sweet secrets, a quirky old plan.
The wall clock just winked, tick-tocking a tune,
As shadows played chess with the light of the moon.

Thoughts flutter like butterflies, chasing my pen,
Writing down jokes from a whimsical den.
With each little quirk, I uncover a laugh,
In the silence of murmurs, it's a quirky giraffe.

Like echoes in whispers, they dance through my skull,
A symphony silent, but never feels dull.
With chuckles and snickers, I find my own way,
In this quiet cacophony where mind games play.

Fertile Ground for Reflection

In the garden of thought, where daisies debate,
A sunflower grumbled, it's all second-rate.
"Why wear sunlight when you could wear a hat?"
Asked a gopher who'd just rolled into that.

Worms with their wisdom planted seeds of delight,
Thoughts sprung up laughing, multiplying overnight.
Tangled in nonsense, the weeds began giggling,
While shadows joined in, their laughter on a wriggling.

Digging deep down, I found chuckles galore,
Each root held a story, each bud had a roar.
As flowers conspired to dance in the grass,
I chuckled at fluff, letting humor amass.

In this fertile ground, absurdity blooms,
Like jesting jokers, they banish the glooms.
With every reflection, I water the cheer,
In the garden of giggles, imagination's dear!

Echoes of Ancient Whispers

In caverns deep, where echoes play,
The poets gather, night 'til day.
They sip on tea, with words so bright,
And dance like shadows in the light.

With quills in hand, they start to scribble,
About the world, so strange and dribble.
A whale in boots, a cat on a bike,
Makes everyone laugh, what a sight!

Ideas flutter like moths in flight,
Chasing stories that feel just right.
A dragon sneezes, the sky turns green,
These jokes are silly, and yet unseen.

So gather 'round, you merry few,
With chocolate rinds and an old shoe.
When words take flight on giggles' wings,
Remember, the laughter that life brings.

Foundations of Lyrical Threads

Once laid down by wise old bards,
With stony chairs and kitchen yards.
They painted dreams on dinner plates,
And hummed aloud to hungry fates.

In a world of wonder, they cooked up rhymes,
With eggs and toast, in awkward climes.
A pickle with flair, a toast of woe,
The laughs from the kitchen are sure to flow.

With every verse, their voices blend,
In laughter's echo, around the bend.
A ghost in a hat sings in the rain,
While pigeons debate if they'll leap the train.

So add a pinch of joy and grace,
Turn the ordinary into a race.
Through mischief and mirth, the song is spun,
These threads of words, a web of fun.

Seeds of Imagination

In gardens bright, where giggles sprout,
The seeds of humor dance about.
A flower yells, "Look at me, hey!"
While the roses chuckle and sway all day.

They planted dreams, not just good vibes,
With hats and shoes and silly jibes.
A gnome on a skateboard whizzes by,
With butterflies laughing as they fly.

With each small seed, a story grows,
Of turtles in tuxedos and silly toes.
The world's a stage, the stage is wild,
With imaginations free, like a playful child.

So come and plant a laugh or two,
In this garden, it's up to you.
The seedlings sprout in colors bright,
As laughter blooms in pure delight.

Essence of Ethereal Rhymes

In realms beyond the silver streams,
Where thoughts take flight on curious dreams.
A unicorn hiccups, piñatas fly,
While fairies debate the best pie supply.

With a sprinkle of stars and a dash of fun,
They weave together the moon and sun.
A walrus sings in a bathtub spree,
While mermaids giggle at the sight of a bee.

These whispers float on cotton clouds,
In absurdity wrapped like silly shrouds.
Through laughter's grace, the verses rise,
Painting love in the bluest skies.

So let your spirit's giggles be free,
In the nature of whimsy, come dance with me.
With strange-shaped rhymes and joyful chimes,
We twirl through life, creating signs.

www.ingramcontent.com/pod-product-compliance
Lightning Source LLC
Chambersburg PA
CBHW051658160426
43209CB00004B/938